MW01249036

Creations By Mit

Art to Make You Smile

A coloring book illustrated by Michele Katz

ISBN-13: 978-1542581103
ISBN-10: 1542581109

***

This book is dedicated to a dear family friend,
Phyllis Benvissuto.
Phyllis, I'm so sorry I did not get it
done sooner, but I hope you are looking down, smiling.
Thank you for the encouragement, support,
and the kick in the pants I needed.

***

For Best Results

For best results, we recommend slipping a piece of cardstock, or
a sheet or two of scrap paper between the page you intend to color
and the following page. This will prevent any bleed-through onto the
next page.

About the Artist

Michele Katz, otherwise known as "Mit" enjoys making people of
all ages smile with her whimsical characters. She earned a BFA in
Illustration from Syracuse University, with a minor in Advertising
Design. She is a published children's book illustrator and proud member
of SCBWI, and is currently working on illustrating her 5th children's
book. Her art can be seen on all sorts of products, ranging from
greeting cards to mouse pads, to coffee mugs. Follow the Creations By
Mit page on both Facebook and Instagram, and visit her Zazzle store
to see more!

www.facebook.com/creationsbymit/
www.instagram.com/creationsbymit/
www.zazzle.com/creationsbymit/

***

TABLE OF CONTENTS

- Air Traffic
- Alley Antics
- Bear Smooch
- Bubble Maker
- Daisy Roll
- Dog Park
- Downhill Fun
- Fish Bowl
- Graffiti Kitty
- Home Sweet Home
- Jungle Tag
- Just Dance
- Knitting Time
- Neckware
- Night Club

***

TABLE OF CONTENTS CONTINUED......

- Nut Case
- On the Scent
- Orchard Raiders
- Rub A Dub Dub
- Smiling Sea
- Splash
- Strawberry Goodness
- Swamp Folk
- Together We Win

***

***

***

***

***

***

***

***

***

***

***

***

***

***

***

***

***

***

***

***

***

***

***

***

***

Made in the USA
Middletown, DE
07 March 2017